FrankSinatra

text **Paula Taylor**
illustrations **John Keely**
design concept **Mark Landkamer**

published by **Creative Education**
Mankato, Minnesota

Published by Creative Educational Society, Inc.,
123 South Broad Street, Mankato, Minnesota 56001
Copyright © 1976 by Creative Educational Society, Inc. International
copyrights reserved in all countries.
No part of this book may be reproduced in any form without written
permission from the publisher. Printed in the United States.
Distributed by Childrens Press,
1224 West Van Buren Street, Chicago, Illinois 60607

Library of Congress Number: 75-34587   ISBN: 0-87191-460-3

1890614

Caesar's Palace

Frank Sinatra is making one of his now-rare personal appearances. His show at Caesar's Palace is billed as the "Greatest Musical Variety Show in Las Vegas History." On opening night, Hollywood celebrities flock to the Palace, followed by reporters. Movie and record company executives stride in. Middle-aged Sinatra fans rub elbows with professional gamblers.

The show is sold out. The 1,100-seat show room is crowded to full capacity. One desperate fan offers the headwaiter $1,000 for a table for two. He is turned away.

At precisely 10:30, the lights dim. The show begins. The acts include the *Fifth Dimension, Jose Feliciano,* and other big-name attractions. But the people in the audience haven't come to see them. It's Sinatra they are all waiting for.

At last, the curtains open wide, revealing the bandleader poised with baton in hand. There is a long roll on the kettle drum. Conversations cease. Finally Frank Sinatra strolls on stage, immaculately dressed as usual, in a dark dinner suit.

He is obviously no longer young. His thin face has filled out, and his cheeks sag a little. His hair is flecked with gray. But he still possesses the air of authority that holds an audience spellbound. Sinatra's hypnotic blue eyes rove over the crowd. A smile briefly twists the corner of his mouth. Finally, he starts singing, "When I was 17 . . . it was a very good year . . ."

Sinatra's famous voice has thinned and deepened a bit, but the old magic is still there. It captivates the audience and carries them back through time — back to the 60's, when mop-haired teen-agers were screaming over the Beatles . . . when rock music dominated the airwaves. But it was Frank Sinatra's dreamy "Strangers in the Night" that soared to the top of the charts.

. . . Back to the 50's, when Elvis Presley was the teen-agers' idol, and the throbbing beat of rock 'n roll came bursting on to the popular music scene . . . when jazz was in retreat. But Frank Sinatra was scoring hits with swinging numbers like "Young at Heart" and "Come Fly With Me."

And, finally . . . back to the 40's, when most of those in the audience were teen-agers, dancing to the swinging rhythms of the big dance bands . . . when Glen Miller, Tommy Dorsey, and Benny Goodman were in their heyday . . . and the girls were swooning over Sinatra himself.

Sinatra goes on singing, taking the audience on a nostalgic swing through 30 years of popular music. To climax the performance, he belts out one of his most electrifying numbers, "The Lady Is a Tramp." Then he bows. The audience, brought suddenly back to the present, rises as one to give him a standing ovation.

Sinatra nods, accepting the thunderous applause graciously but matter-of-factly. For him the show was successful, but routine. He expects capacity crowds, and this politely-applauding audience hardly measures up to the screaming crowds that greeted him back in the 40's. Throwing a kiss to the audience, he saunters off the stage.

In Person

"I don't have any mountains left to climb," says Frank Sinatra. His records sell in the tens of millions. He can appear in movies or on television at phenomenal fees whenever he wants. Although he's known as a popular singer, Sinatra has sung with jazz bands and symphony orchestras. He's also conducted symphonies, even though he's never had a music lesson and doesn't read music.

In a directory of famous people, he lists himself simply as "Sinatra, Frank, baritone." But actually, Sinatra has successfully pursued a variety of careers. He is an Academy Award-winning actor, a film director, and an independent film producer at the Warner Brothers Studio. For years, he hosted his own radio and television programs. He's also proved himself to be an astute businessman. Besides shares in record companies, music publishers, and film-production companies, Sinatra owns hotels, office buildings, apartments, and even a private airline.

The income from his various careers has made Frank Sinatra one of the world's richest men. Money pours in from his far-flung business interests. His salary as an actor averages a quarter of a million dollars per film. A single personal appearance brings him as much as $10,000. He gets a large share of the profits from his hundreds of records and films. In total, Sinatra's income averages around $3.5 million a year.

As a businessman, Sinatra is shrewd but impulsive. On one occasion, he called his lawyer and directed him to buy the Kirkeby Building, a large office complex in Los Angeles. "But it's not for sale," the lawyer protested.

"I want it," insisted Frank.

"Why?" asked the lawyer.

"They won't let me land my helicopter on top,"

Sinatra replied.

Frank enjoys spending money, as well as acquiring it. A few years ago, two of his Hollywood friends celebrated their 25th wedding anniversary. Frank threw a party for them that lasted 72 hours and cost him $25,000.

Sinatra's extravagance is a Hollywood legend. He hands out $250 gold cigarette lighters to mere acquaintances. Family and friends are careful not to wish for things in his presence. One night at a dinner party in Beverly Hills, the daughter of the hostess remarked that she missed the saltwater taffy she used to get in Atlantic City. Three days later, she found her front door blocked by a 50 pound box of the candy, sent air-freight from New Jersey.

Sinatra's desert home in Palm Springs, California, reflects his lavish taste. The kitchen alone cost $100,000. There are two guest houses, private tennis courts, a helicopter landing pad, and a saltwater pool. Music can be heard in every room. When Sinatra is at home, the stereo plays constantly — but not his records. He prefers classical music and is an expert on Berlioz and Puccini. He is also a fine amateur painter.

Sinatra is now almost 60. Several years ago, he announced his retirement. But he doesn't spend much of his time painting or listening to music. He still commutes to his Los Angeles office nearly every day to personally oversee his business interests. He is happiest when he's on the move, wheeling and dealing, recording and performing.

Sinatra is an impatient man. More than anything, he hates to be kept waiting. On movie sets, he paces up and down between takes. If he finds a party boring, he leaves. Commuting to his office through the start-and-stop rush hour traffic on the Los Angeles freeways jangled his

nerves. So he bought a jet helicopter and a private plane. Now he can get to his office in minutes.

Sometimes Frank flies down to Las Vegas with a group of friends for a night on the town. But mostly, he stays at home. Friends often come to visit. Frank is an excellent host who spares no expense to entertain guests royally. Every morning his cook travels to the Los Angeles airport to pick up delicacies flown in especially for Sinatra or his friends.

His taste in food has changed over the years. In the 40's every Sinatra fan knew that Frank's favorite food was a banana split. Now he lunches on prociutto and melon, cheese, and red wine, and orders clams and Italian bread flown in for dinner from his favorite restaurant in New York.

Even though he has many friends, Frank Sinatra is basically a loner. His friends enjoy his hospitality, accept his gifts, and even fly with him around the world; but few feel really close to him. All three of Sinatra's marriages ended in divorce. Now he lives alone.

Frank often has trouble sleeping. Frequently, he is awake until dawn. To pass the time, he reads or works crossword puzzles. Every room of his house is full of books. Frank has read them all, from Shakespeare to cookbooks, science texts to history. Once a friend recommended a book on naval warfare to put Sinatra to sleep. Later, he found Frank had not only read the book but become an expert on the subject.

In the evening, if he doesn't feel like reading, Sinatra often sits for hours in a lounge chair by the side of his pool. Wrapped in blankets against the desert chill, he stares at the stars, waiting for sleep to come. Then, in the quiet hours of the night, memories come flooding back: the good times and the bad, the high hopes and lost loves, the battles he's won and lost.

Sometimes he thinks back to the days when he was a teen-age idol. Smiling to himself, Sinatra remembers the newspaper headlines: "Riot at the Paramount!" "Bobby-soxers Swoon over Sinatra!" He shakes his head, "Those kids were really something! I'll never forget that old swooning business."

Riot at the Paramount

Suddenly it's 1944 again. A younger, leaner Frank Sinatra is being hustled into the Paramount Theatre in New York for a 6:00 a.m. rehearsal. Already thousands of fans are lined up outside. Some girls have been waiting there since the day before.

At 9:00 a.m. as the doors open for the first show, fifty extra ushers struggle to control the frantic mob. Clutching photographs of their idol and wearing copies of his floppy bow tie, fans push and shove their way in. The ticket booth is destroyed in the crush. Nearby shop windows are smashed. Passersby are trampled.

The 3,000-seat theatre is quickly filled to overflowing. While ushers try to clear reluctant teen-agers from the aisles, those lucky enough to claim seats settle down to wait for "The Voice" to appear.

Meanwhile, outside the theatre, the crowd continues to grow. A line of 10,000 fans, six abreast, runs down 43rd Street, snakes along 8th Avenue, and continues down 44th Street. Twenty thousand more fans clog Times Square, stopping all traffic. Calls go out for extra police. By the end of the day, over 700 officers are on hand.

Inside the theatre, there is only slightly less confusion. A movie drags on. The fans ignore it. They chatter, joke,

14

and exchange Sinatra stories. One girl shows an admiring group a bandage on her arm. "That's where Frankie touched me," she explains proudly.

Another fan tells envious listeners of dashing into a restaurant where Sinatra had eaten breakfast and of finishing his half-eaten bowl of cornflakes. Some girls display trophies they have collected: a cigarette butt left by Sinatra in a hotel ashtray, a strand of his hair from the barbershop floor, a piece of a hotel sheet he slept on.

As the movie ends, the air is charged with excitement. "We want Frankie!" the fans yell. Finally, a familiar bar of music sounds. A bony-faced young man in a tweed jacket and brown trousers moves awkwardly toward center stage. The crowd goes crazy. Fans rush toward the stage and are pushed back by determined ushers.

On stage, the young man gestures bashfully to the crowd, trying to quiet them. Finally, he takes the microphone in both hands and starts to sing: "Embrace me, my sweet embraceable you. . ." He smiles tenderly at first one girl, then another.

The fans shriek and moan. Some slump into their seats, overcome with emotion. A few actually faint. When their idol sings that nobody loves him, several hundred girls shout, "No, Frankie, I do." One song after another is drowned out by screams. The audience is quiet only during brief moments when Frank stops singing and threatens to leave the stage.

Suddenly, Sinatra vanishes. The performance is over. Shrieks from the audience rise to a crescendo. To quiet the crowd, the orchestra swings into the "Star Spangled Banner." Twin spotlights focus on the American flag. The ushers look nervous, wondering whether to expect a full-scale riot. But the audience settles down to wait for the next show. Only 250 girls — out of 3,000 — give up their seats and leave the theatre.

All day long, thousands of fans scream through one show after another. The window of Sinatra's dressing room has to be blacked out. Even a glimpse of their hero is enough to send fans outside into hysterics. After the last performance, fans continue milling around the theatre, waiting for Sinatra to appear. But he remains out of sight in his dressing room, waiting for his bodyguard to figure out how to smuggle him safely through mobs of admirers. Finally, hours later, his security men hurry him out a back door into an alley where a taxi is waiting.

Sinatrauma

No singer had ever before touched off such mass hysteria. From New York to California, teen-aged girls turned out by the thousands, screaming and cheering, whenever Sinatra appeared. When he traveled by train, as many as 5,000 fans met him at the station.

Once when Sinatra's plane landed in Detroit, the Secretary of War happened to be passing by in an official limousine, escorted by a police motorcade. When the Secretary noticed the crowd of fans closing in on Sinatra, he told the police escort they'd better take care of the singer instead.

Everywhere he went, Sinatra was trailed by mobs of fans. Whenever he went for a walk in New York, there were such massive traffic jams that police asked him not to linger on city streets. Sinatra tried to disguise himself by wearing dark glasses and a hat, but sharp-eyed fans

spotted him immediately. "Nobody looks from the back like Sinatra does," they said.

Even at home, Sinatra had no privacy. Fans surrounded the house night and day. When the singer looked out a window, he was likely to find himself face to face with young admirers looking in.

Adults were bewildered. They couldn't figure out why Sinatra had such an effect on his fans. Music critics and psychologists, stunned parents and jealous boyfriends were all asking the same question: "What's he got?" They saw nothing special in Sinatra's looks — he was thin and undersized, with hollow cheeks and ears that were too big.

Some people dismissed the fans' hysterics as a publicity stunt. "Purely mass psychology built up by his press agent," they insisted. Others argued that World War II was responsible for the fans' strange behavior. They thought it was due to the loneliness of millions of single girls whose boyfriends were in service overseas. An English critic thought it was Sinatra's shy smile that worked the magic on his audience.

Few members of the older generation bothered to listen to what teen-agers were saying about Sinatra. But it was one of his fans who probably offered the best explanation of their behavior. She said, "Frankie has a certain something that makes every girl feel he's singing to her — and to her alone."

Through the years, almost all Sinatra's listeners have felt this kind of intimate relationship with him. For his teen-aged audiences in the 40's, it was a new experience. No other popular singer had such an intimate way with a song.

In an interview many years later, Frank tried to explain

his extraordinary ability to involve an audience in the mood of a song. "I think it's because I'm involved myself," he said. "It's not something I do deliberately; I can't help myself. If the song is a lament at the loss of love, I get an ache in my gut; I feel the loss myself, and I cry out the loneliness, the hurt, and the pain that I feel."

In the 40's, popular singers rarely expressed their emotions honestly and directly the way Sinatra did. When they sang of pain or loneliness, other singers didn't seem to feel hurt or lonely themselves. Sinatra was different. He was involved. He reached out to his listeners with his eyes, his hands, and his voice. He made an audience feel as deeply as he did. He never sang *for* his listeners; he always sang *to* them.

Loner

Frank has always tried to reach out to other people. In Hollywood, he has become known for his generosity. "He's the biggest soft touch in history," one friend says of him. "If he ever got paid back all that's owed him, he could settle the national debt."

Whenever he hears someone is in trouble, Frank is there to help. Once, an actor he knew only slightly had a heart attack. When Frank heard the man was nearly bankrupt, he not only paid his hospital bills but came to visit him every day to cheer him up. It was a typical gesture. Colleges and hospitals, as well as all sorts of unfortunate people, have received help from Frank Sinatra, much of it anonymous.

Such generosity is easy for Frank, but lasting relationships with people seem to elude him. Frank is a loyal friend but a demanding one. A great many people don't measure up to his expectations. One after another, his three marriages — to Nancy Barbato, his childhood sweetheart; to Ava Gardner, a Hollywood movie star; and to Mia Farrow, a young actress — all have ended in divorce.

Over the years, Sinatra's domestic battles have been given wide publicity in newspaper gossip columns. So have his fights with friends, reporters, movie producers, T.V. cameramen, and anyone else who happens to criticize him.

"As a singer, there's no one like him," says a record producer who worked with Sinatra for many years; "but as a guy, there is no one more difficult to handle. Each time you saw Frank, it was like meeting a different guy. How he treated you depended solely on how he felt at *that* moment and what was bugging him . . . He was so appealing at times he could charm butterflies — and then again, so miserable he could bother a snake."

Sinatra's constantly changing moods make him a difficult man to work for. On location for a movie, he once let loose a torrent of insults at a prop boy who had forgotten to bring a chair to his dressing room. Later, he felt ashamed. "Remember that prop boy I yelled at a few minutes ago?" he said to one of the stage hands. "I understand his wife is sick. Send her flowers, and make sure we pay all the medical bills."

Sometimes Sinatra's violent temper could be dangerous. When he was singing with Tommy Dorsey's band, Frank got angry at the drummer, Buddy Rich. He felt the

20

drummer was showing off during his vocal solos. After one performance, Sinatra picked up a pitcher of water and threw it at Rich. Fortunately, the drummer ducked. The heavy pitcher hit the wall so hard that pieces of glass stuck in the plaster. Afterwards, Frank was all apologies. When Rich left the orchestra to form his own band, Sinatra helped him out with a $25,000 loan.

Frank never ignored an insult levied at him. Once while he was singing, a heckler in the audience yelled, "You stink." Sinatra stopped the band, walked over to the table, and challenged the tipsy gentleman to a fight. The man stared at Sinatra for a moment, then shook his head. Frank marched back on stage and resumed the show.

Sometimes his opponent didn't back down. On one occasion, Sinatra got into a fist fight with a newspaper columnist who took the matter to court. Frank was ordered to pay the columnist a $9,000 settlement.

Flashback

In later years, Frank Sinatra tried hard to change his brawler image. He dressed with impeccable taste. He associated with members of high society and even entertained the President at his luxurious desert home. He tried hard to control his temper. But sometimes he couldn't resist using his fists to settle an argument. It's not surprising, considering his background.

In Hoboken, New Jersey, where Sinatra grew up, fist fights were tame. Teen-aged gangs fought with broken bottles and tire chains. Frank still has scars from the fights he was involved in.

Neighbors remember him as a lonely boy who didn't have many friends. Frank always felt different from other children. In the Italian neighborhood where he grew up, families of 12 were common. But Frank was an only child.

His father, Martin Sinatra, was a small, silent man who worked long hours as a bartender. Dolly Sinatra, Frank's mother, was said to be the only person in the neighborhood who could make sense of the many different Italian dialects spoken there. She was deeply involved in politics and had been elected a Democratic ward leader.

In the Sinatras' neighborhood, other kids' mothers were always home. Frank's mother rarely was. Frank was left in the care of his grandmother. He spent much of his time alone, leaning over his grandmother's garden gate, staring into space.

Hoboken was a grimy port city of shipyards and factories, railroad yards and bars. Music was rarely heard, except in church. There were no musical instruments in the Sinatra home. Frank never had a music lesson. He got his musical education by listening closely to performers he admired.

When Frank was a teen-ager, Bing Crosby was his idol. He spent hours listening to Bing on the radio. When he was 18, Frank went to hear Crosby in person at a theatre in Jersey City. He left the performance determined to become a famous singer — as famous as Bing.

For six long years, the only jobs Frank could get were meager ones. He sang in small, dingy nightclubs for as little as $3.00 a night. His parents tried to persuade him to go back to school. They wanted him to learn a trade so that he could get a steady job. But Frank wouldn't give up.

His determination finally paid off. Harry James, a trumpet player who had left Benny Goodman's orchestra and was forming a band of his own, asked Sinatra to be his vocalist. With the James band, Frank made several records. One of them came to the notice of Tommy Dorsey, who had one of the top dance bands in the country. Dorsey happened to be looking for a new vocalist. He hired Frank.

Apprenticeship

At first Frank Sinatra seemed to be just another pleasant-voiced band singer. He sounded much like Bing Crosby. So did most of the other young singers. Crosby was still the top male vocalist in the country. Everyone had tried to copy his style. But Frank didn't want to sound like anyone else. "It occurred to me," he said later, "that maybe the world didn't need *another* Crosby. I decided to experiment a little and come up with something different."

Frank began listening carefully to the musicians around him. He particularly admired Tommy Dorsey's trombone playing. When Tommy played, the melody flowed on endlessly, smooth and unbroken. The trombonist never seemed to take a breath. Fascinated, Frank began watching Tommy closely. Finally he discovered a tiny hole in the corner of the trombonist's mouth where he was actually breathing at the same time the sound was being carried through his horn.

Excited at his discovery, Frank wondered if a singer could do somewhat the same thing. After a lot of practice, he found he could. Instead of the 3 or 4 bars of music most singers could manage, he was able to sing as many as 6 or 8 bars without taking an audible breath. This gave his singing the same flowing, unbroken quality as Dorsey's trombone-playing.

Sinatra also studied the way other singers handled the microphone. He began to think of the mike as an instrument which he could play in the same way as an instrumentalist might play a violin or a trombone. He learned when to turn toward it and when to move away. He learned to hear exactly what the microphone picked up and adjust his singing so that he sounded even better with the mike than without it. To most singers, the microphone was a liability. Sinatra made it an asset.

Frank learned from other singers, too. He often dropped in at New York's 52nd Street club where Billie Holiday sang. He admired Billie both for her singing and for her refusal to give up fighting against poverty and racial discrimination. Night after night, Frank listened to Billie pour out all her bitterness and sadness in song. He began to try to convey the same depth of emotion in his own singing.

Solo

Frank's experimenting began to pay off. He no longer sounded like anyone else. He had created a style of singing uniquely his own. The nuances in his voice were like contrasting colors in a painting. The way he spaced words gave the lyrics of a song new meaning. Music critics began remarking about Frank Sinatra's vocal artistry. Audiences responded just as enthusiastically.

Tommy Dorsey's band made a number of records with Sinatra as the featured soloist. Many were hits. But at

24

first, people didn't know who was singing the solos. Dorsey's records were labeled only with the orchestra's name. Letters began pouring into the RCA Victor offices asking who the soloist was. Finally, Tommy yielded and allowed Frank's name to be added to future record labels.

As Sinatra became more and more popular, his name on the records got larger and Dorsey's got smaller. Tommy was not happy to find that his vocalist was becoming more popular than he was. Arguments between the two became more bitter. Finally, Frank left the band to try to make it on his own.

A few months later, Frank got a booking at the Paramount Theatre in New York. He was to appear with Benny Goodman's band as an "extra added attraction." To the surprise of the theatre management, the "added attraction" created more excitement than the famous dance band. When Frank came on stage, the audience went wild. Each performance drew larger and noisier crowds of teen-agers. Newspapers picked up the story. At the end of the Paramount engagement, Frank Sinatra found himself a national celebrity.

At a time when record sales of a few thousand copies were considered respectable, Sinatra's records sold in the millions. Film companies competed with one another to sign Sinatra for movies. In most films, Frank made only walk-on appearances. But his name alone was enough to sell the pictures to the public.

Sinatra made personal appearances at the best hotels and nightclubs all across the country. He was even booked for performances with several major symphony orchestras. When Sinatra sang at the symphony, concerts were invariably sold out. Usually-sedate audiences whistled and cheered.

26

For almost six years, Sinatra rode high on a wave of incredible popularity. But in the late 40's, taste in popular music began changing. One after another, the big dance bands faded from the scene. The lush rhythms of the big bands were replaced by the insistent beat of smaller rhythm and blues, and country groups. Frank Sinatra found that his romantic ballads were out of style.

Sales of Sinatra's records dropped off. His recording contract was not renewed. Attendance at his performances dropped off sharply. Girls no longer swooned in the aisles when Sinatra appeared on stage. The teenagers had found other idols. Most people thought Frank Sinatra was finished as a singer.

Then in 1953, Sinatra again burst onto the entertainment scene. This time he made a hit as an actor, playing the part of Maggio, a tough little Italian-American soldier in the movie *From Here to Eternity.* His performance won him an Academy Award. It also won him a flood of offers for film roles — this time not as a bit player, but as a serious actor. In quick succession, Sinatra played a variety of difficult parts, convincing even the most doubtful critics that he could act, as well as sing.

Most people were surprised at Sinatra's acting talent, but to him it didn't seem strange. "There's no reason why a singer can't go dramatic," he said. "A singer is essentially an actor." Song lyrics had always been important to Sinatra. He felt that a good song always told a story, just as a play did, and that a good singer conveyed a feeling of drama to an audience.

Sinatra's success in films sparked new interest in his singing. Sales of his records suddenly sky-rocketed. He was deluged with offers for personal appearances and television shows. By 1955, Sinatra was even more popular

than he'd been in the 40's. The star was exploding into a superstar.

A Man and His Music

In 1965 Frank Sinatra celebrated his 50th birthday. The press and the television networks joined in the celebration. That year Sinatra's picture appeared on the covers of three of the country's biggest news magazines. CBS and NBC presented television documentaries telling the story of Sinatra's 25 years in show business.

The magazine articles and television programs recalled the highlights of Sinatra's long career — his growing popularity as a band singer, the hysteria of the 40's, his decline and magnificent comeback, his wealth, his hit records and Academy Awards. The many tributes presented a picture of the man the public knew. But there was another side of him they did not touch.

Frank Sinatra is a complicated person. He is a superstar — confident, wealthy, successful. But he is also a man who is familiar with heartache and loneliness, a man who worries about getting old, a man who sits alone at night, looking at the stars.

Sinatra does not often talk about this side of himself. In fact, through the years he has battled reporters to keep them from prying into his private life. In the 50's, he built a secluded retreat in a canyon in Beverly Hills. A high, barbed-wire fence surrounded the property. On the gate, a blunt notice greeted visitors: "If you haven't been invited, you better have a damn good reason for ringing this bell." But careful as he was to keep his private life hidden from the curious, Sinatra revealed his innermost thoughts and feelings in another way — in his music.

The man his songs disclosed was often quite different from his public image. After his success in *From Here to Eternity,* Frank was outwardly confident and exuberant. "Man, I feel 8 feet tall," he told one reporter. "Everything is ahead of me. I'm on top of the world."

Yet at the same time he was telling everyone how happy he was, Frank was agonizing over his private problems: the breakup of his marriage to Ava Gardner, his self-doubt, his loneliness. He didn't mention his troubles to anyone, but the melancholy songs he was recording, "It's a Blue World," "There Will Never Be Another You," "I'll Never Smile Again," reveal the way he was feeling.

Frank Sinatra once called himself an "18-karat manic depressive who's lived a life of violent emotional contradictions." Sinatra's mercurial temperament may have made him difficult to work with and to live with, but it lies at the heart of his success as an artist. It has given him the ability to feel both sadness and elation with great intensity and to communicate his feelings to an audience.

Other singers have tried to imitate Sinatra, but none have succeeded; for Frank Sinatra's style and his personality are one and the same. Both the man and his music are unique.

JACKSON FIVE   NEIL DIAMOND
CARLY SIMON   CAROLE KING
BOB DYLAN   DIANA ROSS
JOHN DENVER   THE OSMONDS
THE BEATLES   CHARLIE RICH
ELVIS PRESLEY   ELTON JOHN
JOHNNY CASH   CHICAGO
CHARLEY PRIDE   FRANK SINATRA
ARETHA FRANKLIN   BARBRA STREISAND
ROBERTA FLACK   OLIVIA NEWTON-JOHN
STEVIE WONDER

Rock'n PopStars